A Ray of Hope

Stacey Llewellyn

To order additional copies of this book, contact:
Xlibris
844-714-8691
www.Xlibris.com
Orders@Xlibris.com

ISBN:	Softcover	978-1-6641-5548-0
	Hardcover	978-1-6641-5549-7
	EBook	978-1-6641-5547-3

Print information available on the last page

Rev. date: 01/29/2021

Contents

Introduction   1

Love   2

Honestly Speaking   4

How Could It Be?   6

Good Food   8

Winning   10

The Gist of Things   12

It's Simple   14

Finances   16

The Very Best of Me   18

Smile Often   20

Beautiful Rocks   22

What Is Anger?   24

You Are Every Mother's Dream   26

Until You Are Mine   28

Night Sky   30

I Dream   32

Dear Future Me   34

Gossip   36

Am Addicted   38

Crimson   40

I Planned   42

Dancing   44

Who Will?   46

Night Love   48

Through My Eyes   50

Fly Guy   52

Personal Use Only   54

Star   56

Twisted   58

Hello   60

The Power of Love   62

Don't Touch   64

Introduction

I hope this book can brighten your day and give you a sense of pulling through those dark days. Hopefully it gives you a ray of hope that bad times are only momentary and that a rainbow always comes after a storm not before, and as long as there is life, there`s always hope

Love

Today I discover a strange feeling, a longing, a yearning that one could describe as a flutter or a shiver not in the eerie, condescending way that often depicts a horror movie, imagined with as much clarity that has fundamentally shifted my years of ideals.

Is this truly what **love** is?

The unprecedented, unwavering passion that cannot be altered or dismissed as one does with an old broken toy or discarded broken glass!

Can a broken heart truly be repaired?

Is the notion of true **love** merely a myth, or are we so scared of being powerless to the ruling of humanity that we create an illusion of **love** to block us ever truly being in **love**? Firstly with ourselves, secondly others. As I stated, to be in **love** is to be weak and powerless to an extent as **love** is the most powerful force that governs the universe, so it's a force to be reckoned with.

As we will never truly comprehend its magnitude as we are often not open to love, what is the real representation of love?

Truly we all have some prefixed disposition or notion about the true concept of love,

Far from what the real power of love truly is,

it's the key to the universe, not just the human heart but the very basis of all creation. **Love** is not to be toyed with! It really is a thin line between love and hate that should not be tampered with or altered as it can have dire effects and impact. Significantly it is in a way you could not make sense to a person that has never felt real love.

Not to scare you, **love** is wonderful and a real blessing that is to be cherished as a gift that gives and enriches your very essence, the gift that keeps on giving. **Love.**

Honestly Speaking

Honesty speaks that which is thought the voices that go soft and unsaid are the ones that you know deep down inside, that speaks to you over your pride that still inner voice that you cannot hide as much as you try to bury it as much as you do everything to keep busy to preoccupy yourself with all the many distractions

When all is said and done, it creeps up on you like a voice in the night

Quit the bull and look within

Your conscience is there; it can't hide as much as you pretend

That's why guilt in your mind can never truly hide, in constant love you must abide

To come over the tide

Joy is what you have always never forgotten that you can and will

So tired of being used and abused by the people I love

Love is not to hurt like this I loved more than I love me

Now I all feel is anger for the way I allowed myself to be used. I stopped being a slave to my heart

I will be me a loving, kind person that means that my limits are set that I give I live, but you will never hurt me again like that; you fool me once never goanna fool me twice. You are not worthy of such pure a heart. You ripped it apart, the love of god is putting it together again.

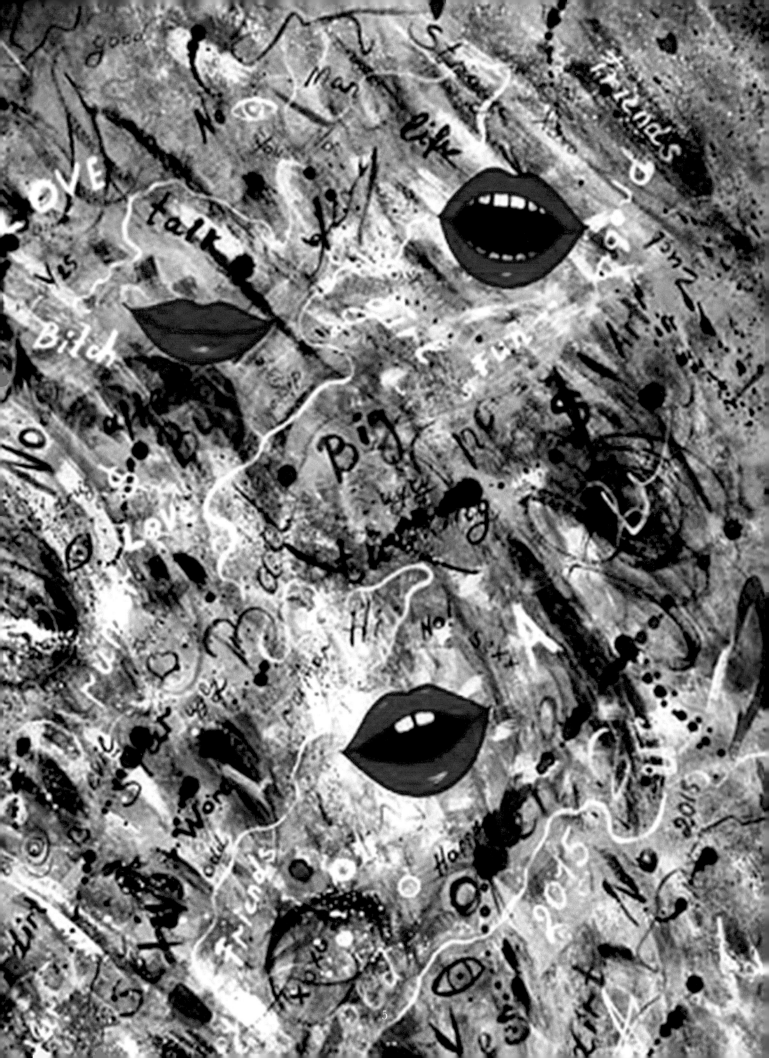

How Could It Be?

I often wonder if not ponder on nature's evergreens

How could it be?

As I face some of the most challenging times of my life

I find comfort and hope looking at these silent masters

most have withstood the world's greatest storms

They stand the test of time

They stand through blizzards

They stand through the ice age

They stand through drought

They stand through disease

They stand through heat waves

They stand through wars

They stand flourishing strongly, silently and evergreen as the sun shimmers rays of light

They stand beautiful

it is such a hope they have faced all life's challenges and are still able to stand so I take heart and hope as they stand so can I silent yet strong, beautiful with grace that as they face and pass life's greatest test I will to!

Be able to flourish with such grace after all they face

Good Food

Good food speaks beyond the barriers of language

Beyond race, beyond geographical place

Beyond time and space as recipes transcend the limits of time passed on from generation to generation

Each family has its own unique family mix of herbs and spices and intricate kirks that makes food delectably nice and just rightly spiced

Good food is just good food

It knows no bounds

It unties what tides and language divide

Good food is just good food

Ensaladas, linguine, tiramisu, creamy chicken pot pie, and oxtail

Good food is just good food

Good food is delicious and often nutritious so bon appétit

Let us sit down and just eat some good food that as they say in Louisiana that soul food

That good food just like Mama used to make, enjoy

Good food

Winning

Winning and losing, what do you think it is? My notion of that has changed throughout my journey and these passing days.

Winning and losing sometimes does not have any meaning, because

Some people win by losing

And some people lose by winning

Understanding is much deeper than knowledge because there are many people who have knowledge but lack understanding, so many might have knowledge of you but very few that truly understand you!

Some people lose because they truly fear success. I mean winning a personal goal is not easy when you are the reason behind your biggest failures truth be told

You must fear less, hope more

Honesty speaks in the inner thought so listen to yourself more, seek advice when you are unsure there are no discrepancies no contradictions in thought or action when you look deep within in your heart to focus on your goals to free yourself from doubt and disbelief

If you believe in your dreams, you can achieve the unthinkable!

First dream the undreamable, win the battle deep within, then and only then will you win all the challenges along the zig and zag of life's twists and turns; there are many obstacles along life's road, so to ensure your success, you must constantly mot test yourself to ensure you are not the biggest problem holding you back from ultimate success! Ensure you win by winning you.

The Gist of Things

Just because the past did not turn out how you wanted it to

It doesn't mean the future can't be better than you could have ever imagined

If you are not willing to look stupid running with your dreams, then nothing great will ever happen to you apart from the norm

Don't let what you can't do stop you

From doing what you can do

If you are not willing to invest your time, your effort into chasing your dreams, that's all they will ever be

Just an idea, just a thought! Don't be faint-hearted; history is steeped with great inventors that had an idea, that had a dream!

The difference then is that they ran with it!

They did not stop with just the thought of their idea, they ran with it! Till it was clear for all to see! It went from being a thought . . .

to a discussion, from a discussion to a prototype, from a prototype to an invention used by the world today. If they did not risk the thought of looking stupid, then some of history's greatest inventions might not be so! Don't be scared to risk the unusual, run with your deepest goals. Will you have to settle for the ordinary and history might just miss another great invention

So just run with your dream and don't lose steam

It's Simple

Life is simple so why try to complicate it with all the confusion of the world! Why allow fear, doubt, and despair to overwhelm your soul, alter your natural being

Do not feel alone . . . Don't be afraid

At times we all have to be happy being alone; loving yourself is the key to being able to love being you, truly yourself and being happy in your own skin! Loving others, also loving you "Love thy neighbor as you love yourself."

The ways you want to be treated by someone else, treat yourself that way; first lead by example. How can you expect others to value you if you don't show what you value; you do what you can to be good to you. Do healthy things that make you completely happy with yourself. Love you.

Finances

I do not wish (women) to have power over men but over themselves

My goals, to have financial freedom and absolute liberation from the savage life of financial dependence

Loving my thought, me, just how much my financial independence means to me:

Being able to do what I will, when I will without needing to think of being a burden to another living soul!

Not feeling like a charity case or an obligated slave!

Not putting up with being treated substandard or less of a human being because of my lack of secure finances ever again is my main force inside me; after all I have been through in life, I got fed up and sick of being treated like crap because of money or lack of it!

I decided that I had enough and enough is enough. I drew a line in the sand, that I will never again be poor!

they say everything starts in the mind, so I start in my mind, so I start thinking of being rich. I start doing the things I want to, look at the things I need to enable me. I stop limiting myself based on my finances. I started aiming higher than my wallet: some would say I'm mad for thinking that way, but I did it anyway I start to see that only my mind can thoroughly free me. I was only poor as long as in my mind I thought I'm poor!

when you think poor, you make poor decisions; you settle for less than you are worth! In thinking rich, I finally found myself worth it. I started making rich (wise) decisions. In turn my life started to change for the better. I started to attract the things I wanted in my life and stop wasting time, effort, and energy on things I don't want and started to spend it on the things I do want! I started to fix all that I needed to fix one at a time. I made a list, my must-do-get-rich list tailored just for me. I stuck to it no matter what, come rain or shine. I knew that life can be divine, just got to start; it's all in your mind so I started proclaiming my million before I started even earning my first dime. I kept on working on my list, constantly tick, fix, hit, and miss; the results will manifest in time. I will never again be poor. Of this I am certainly sure.

The Very Best of Me

The very best of me just me

I can't be anyone else so I learned to love myself, me just me, the very best of me

What others are blind to see the very best of me?

There's more to me than the average eyes can see

There's more to me than words can describe

I am like an onion with many intricate layers

The very best of me is what I hide because I am tired of all the selfish, jealous lies and all these spiteful eyes that see me as anything and never know who I truly I am

I stopped hoping that people would see just how good, loving me could be. I stopped searching for love

I got the best of me and it's all for me it's me, it's all mine so I know

It's the best of me at the worst of times!

I try to give the best of me

No matter what I have overcome, all said and done

All that I have . . . I muster every ounce of hope! Every ounce of joy, every ounce of optimism, I have in the fiber of my being to be able to give the best of me when there is no rest for me

It true when they say a smile speaks a thousand words

We all have a Mona Lisa-like smile

I put it on like a paint. I wear it like a fake. I used to be able to hide all the worst emotions behind my Mona Lisa; now it's not so easy

Now I really have to dig deep and bring up and out the best of me

Just to get past the worst of times in my life, the testing and pressures of life have worn at me but still after the tears and fears

I put on my Mona Lisa smile and start again

Smile Often

A Smile often hides a lot

I smile even when I cry

I smile even when I feel like I want to break down from all this pain and stress not knowing what comes next

I smile when I feel pain beyond human comprehension

I smile when my body is aching like it is breaking

I smile when I am so overwhelmed I know not how to perceive just how I was deceived

I smile when the anger from my betrayal and the depth in which it took a hold of me, is it really? I smile hoping to awaken from this painful dream, but then I realize that it is not a dream, it's just my waking nightmare. I smile even more than I ever smiled before

My Mona Lisa smile has lasted me more than a mile of this journey of this ordeal

To the point that I often get misunderstood because I am smiling through the worst of . . . just to bring out the best of me I smile even when I cry uncontrollably because I am me

I can be no other but me so I smile because that is just me

So listen to my words and not my appearance because it may deceive you at times

My Mona Lisa smile is perfected like a fine art; my smile hides more than you will ever think

it's my pains, my fears, my joys, and hopes, my ugly-duckling syndrome, my misunderstood emotions, all gift wrapped and presented in a beautiful smile. My Mona Lisa smile contains this much. I smile, I smile, I smile.

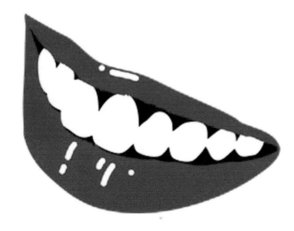

Beautiful Rocks

Beautiful rocks a smile

Beautiful rocks a posh exterior, like how the sedimentary rocks are made

Like water cascades

Beautiful rocks are formed and made through years of molding to be formed

Much like me and the beauty that each year adds a new layer to my depth and the intricate way in which I am made up of all my many layers

Formed for a purpose

Beautiful rocks are a lot like me there's more to them than what eyes can see

So when you see a beautiful rock, please think of me

Beautiful rocks!

What Is Anger?

A Google search stated, "anger is a strong emotion feeling annoyance, displeasure or hastily."

But to say am angry never fits those words, I am not hostile nor am I annoyed. I just don't understand why you never love in a way in which I perceive as love.

To be the way I want to be loved, no confusion, no games, no pain for my heart to never be strained, to never rattle my brain

The way I want to be loved, I feel as if you do not understand me, like I am an alien the way I perceive love to be; in comparison to the love I receive, I am not angry nor am I enraged which lasts for days

Just by what scale do you judge your love? I stay to myself a lot because I can see the heart of men, and your heart is almost untouchable to me, so I sit and wait to hope for faith to intervene

You Are Every Mother's Dream

Perfect fingers

Perfect toes

A perfect cute little nose

You are Every mother's dream; I love the skin you are in

You are every mother's dream, your perfect eyes that sparkle with delight

I can see you smiling through your perfect eyes you are perfect in every single way

You need to know that you are perfect in every way

You are every mother's wish

You are perfect

You are every mother's wish!

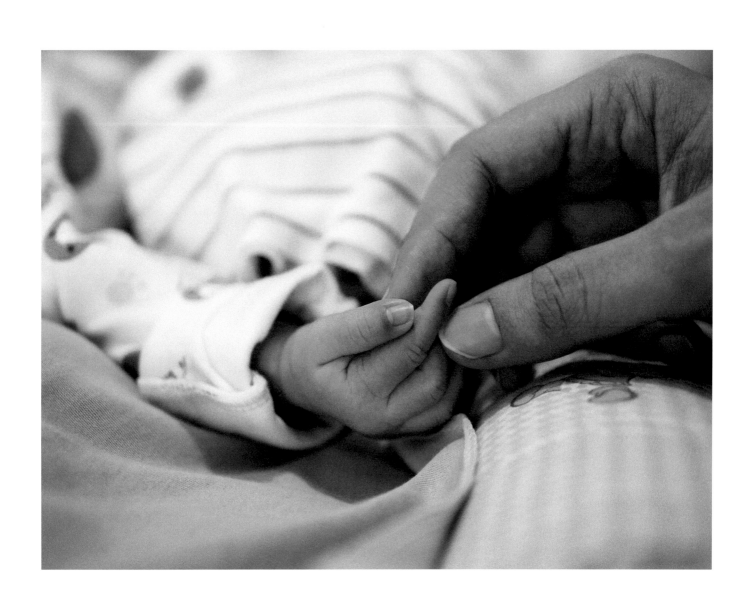

Until You Are Mine

Until you are mine, I will perfect me being the best me that I can be

Until you are mine, I will do all I can to be the me that I can be!

Until you are mine, I will give my best even at the worst of times

Until you are mine, I will always sparkle and shine

Until you are mine, I will try my best to hold you dear in my heart

So space and time can intertwine

Until you are mine, I will delight myself with my perfection

Until you are mine, I will hold you in my thoughts, keep you in my mind

Until you are mine!

Night Sky

A glimmer, a glisten as the night sky is my new day as I bask in the moonlit rays

The stars that shine ever so brightly as the kiss the sky so pretty I feel

Like I can fly above all the years of tears

Above all the nights of loneliness

Above all my fears

Above all my past hurts as I gaze at the splendor that is the night sky

Such beauty and grace

As I look above, I feel the moon's love as I look at the night sky

I Dream

I dream of you and it makes me smile, if only for a while

See your style as finesse as you've mentally undressed me

Got me waiting for you to caress me

See you got beneath my hard exterior which was for my protection

Now you got me in every direction; now I only crave you the most until the day that I'm a ghost

I crave your love and affection; see it's easy to be hard in anger, but I melt like butter when it touches heat

You make my heart flutter in ways words cannot describe

I dream of us together

I dream of us and it makes me happy

I dream of a future with you by my side

I dream . . .

Dear Future Me

Dear future me,

I hope in the next ten years, you would have grown beyond what is shown

I hope you would have learned beyond the lessons on a classroom syllabus so much so you can teach the youngers how to rise and not strive

I hope you will be fulfilled and happy if not just content with time well spent doing good, turning sorrow into joy, I hope you will show love and not hate

I hope you finally find your faith not doubt, I hope you believe in a greater fate not just watching time and date

And that nothing can bend your mind, that time is a healer, and that you're better not bitter

Dear future me

gossip

Is it gossip or constructive criticism?

When you cut me down with your words, when you dash my dreams away with your words that cut like a knife

With words rooted in spite

Is it gossip or constructive criticism?

When you belittle my accomplishments and downplay my attributes

Is it gossip, constructive criticism, or just plain jealousy?

When you create a story just to villainize me

Is it gossip or constructive criticism?

When you kick me when I am down?

Well is it?

Am Addicted

To your love it's like a drug, that was sent from above

It melts even the coldest hearts and sets us apart I knew I loved you right from the start

Am addicted to the feeling of flying when I'm high on your love it's like a drug it gives me wings and makes me fly; when I think of love, it gives me hope on the darkest days

It wipes away years of pain and uncontrollable tears, it turns sorrow into joy

Love is the divine food sent from the gods like the golden ambrosia

Love is truly the food of the gods; love is all you need to heal all my wounds

I'm addicted to your love like a drug it got me wanting more and more

Your love is all I want; your love is all I crave

I want you for my friend, I need for my lover, I want us to last for infinity and beyond

I want, no, I need your love forever; am addicted to you!

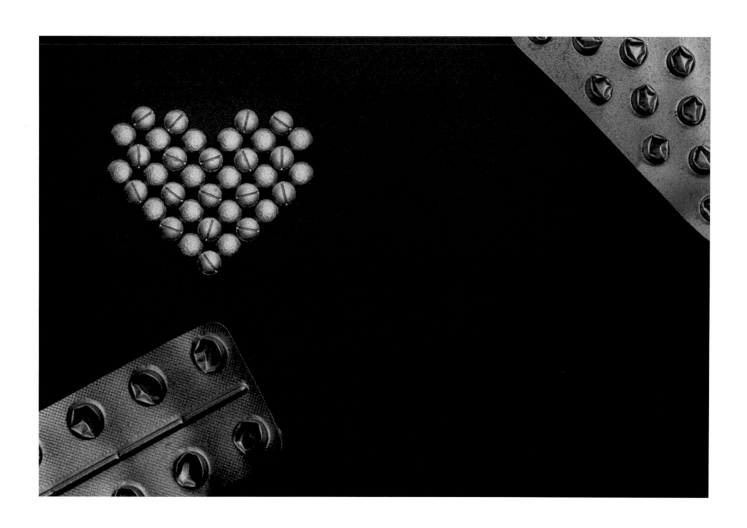

Crimson

As I bathe in the crimson mists that flow as it glows

Gushing from a spring bit, erupts from the mist I twist

In its warm glow, as it showers me, I bask in the crimson rain

I feel invigorated by the warmth of the crimson mist

I dance as entranced by its mesmerizing glow

as I circumnavigate time and fate

I made a star-crossed date. I promise never to be late to your gate; it's a star-studded date, call it faith

I Planned

I planned a life with you in mind

I thought our paths were forever entwined

At the thought of losing, I damn near lost my mind

See I planned for us for you and me

I never planned a you without me; that's a future I can't bear to see

You will never know how much you mean to me

I am made for you and you are made for me

I planned for you, you're irreplaceable to me you see

I will never give your love away

So now you see there's no other for me but you

You are my dearest treasure, my love goes beyond measure

I planned to love you till my dying day I

Planned!

Dancing

Dancing is power

Movement is key, it sets you free

It frees the mind and entrances the body

It makes your soul feel at peace

When I dance, I feel like I got diamonds at the meeting of my thighs

I love the way the symphony entices me with such a sweet melody

I fall under music's spell as a great man once said, "When the music hits, you feel no pain."

I will dance away my sorrows

I will dance away my fears

I will dance away my tears

I will dance till I am in a trance

I will dance, I will dance, I will dance

Who Will?

Who will give a voice to the voiceless?

Who will rise strongly for the weak?

Who can't sleep or sleep?

Who will give a voice to the broken?

Who has cried till their tears are dry?

Who will give love to the broken and ill-treated?

Who will show love and care?

Who will?

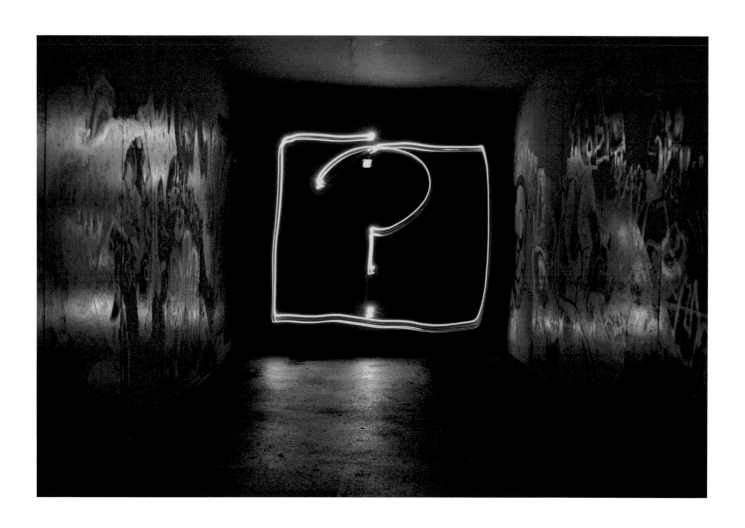

Night Love

When the sun goes to sleep, my lover awakes

The moon starts leaping and gleaming.

Dancing across the sky, the stars witness its beauty

The oceans are drawn like magnet.

I am entranced by its tantalizing beauty.

And his majestic grace as I race for a glance of his beauty.

Mesmerizing beauty, inhaling his love from above

The night sky, my lover, my friend with me till my very end

Through My Eyes

I wonder if you see what I see or what I feel

I smile looking at the room

Smiling at all my pains as my mind is perplexed by the constant flashbacks as I recount

Flashes of a past rooted in pain,

I smile, can you see the pain in my voice? The sorrow in my eyes?

As I try to be like everyone else, I feel so odd.

Will I feel like this forever? Will sorrow never leave me to enjoy life without the painful past flashing by every so often, looming its ugly head, giving my hurtful woes, trying to open old wounds when will I heal?

Can you see what I see?

Can you see through my smile?

Can you see through my eyes?

Can you see what I see?

A broken heart, afraid to trust, can I let you in or will you just hurt me?

Can you see what I see a person who is scared to trust!

Can you see what I see when I look at me?

Fly Guy

Hey, fly guy,

You catch my eye,

From across the room,

I like your style and your smile,

I dance so you can see me,

Do you like what you see?

Hey, fly guy, I admire your style,

Do you see me in the crowded room?

Hey, fly guy, does you see me looking at you.

Watching you watching me!

Hey, fly guy!

Personal Use Only

Like your toothbrush,

Am for your use only

Like your razor,

Am for your use only

Like your intimate possession

Am for your use only

I'm completely at your disposal

I am for your use only

Let me be your entertainer, your doctor, your chef, your friend, your lover

Am for your use only

Star

On this day a star was born,

Blessed among men and I love you

You shine so brightly, you know no war

You know no strife, you're perfect in every way

You gave me hope, when my hope was gone

I am blessed to have held you

Am blessed to have known you

You're forever a shining star

I love you so much my shining star

I will praise you still

My shining star

Twisted

To all the pains that made me thought that life was sometimes twisted

What was meant to break me only made me

That I can look, and that damn I am gifted

Through it all, I still wear a smile that has lasted more than a mile of this journey

I sit and sometimes reflect for a while,

like a little child, I learned that sometimes a loss is really a win

twisted I know but life goes on that is for sure

twisted!

Hello

Hello, my friend

Hello, my dear

Hello, my one and only

Hello, I want you near to me always

Counting down the hours, minutes, and days

Till I see your face just to say

Hello, my love

I hold you dear to my heart, you're my joy

My dearest friend,

Hello! Hello! Hello!

The Power of Love

Love is a powerful force that can change your life

For the better if you welcome it into your heart

Without fear of being hurt

To love like you've never been hurt

I wish I could forget the pain to truly love again to love like I never been hurt

'Cause love frees you, but I am very cautious; you're not to blame

For what he did, that's why I love you

You made me feel things I could never explain, such joy beyond what I can measure

Your love is a power that surpasses all other; you mend all the broken parts of my heart, your

Love is like pure power. It races through my veins and makes me feel whole again

Love is truly powerful

Don't Touch

Don't touch me please

I beg you please I don't know you

Don't touch me please

I don't want to be touched by a stranger

Don't touch me please

I don't belong to you

Don't touch me please

Am not a toy to be fondled

Don't touch me please I don't

Know you if you touch without my consent

I will destroy you! Don't say I never warned you

Don't touch me please

Printed in the United States
By Bookmasters